PRAYERS
Women
S0-ADD-717

Compiled by MariLee Parrish.

ISBN 978-1-60260-193-2



Some material previously published in *365 Moments of Adventure for Girlfriends*, *365 Everyday Prayers*, and *365 Prayers for Women*, published by Barbour Publishing.



Published by Barbour Publishing, Inc., P.O. Box 719, Uhrichsville, Ohio 44683, www.barbourbooks.com

*Our mission is to publish and distribute inspirational products offering exceptional value and biblical encouragement to the masses.*

Printed in China.

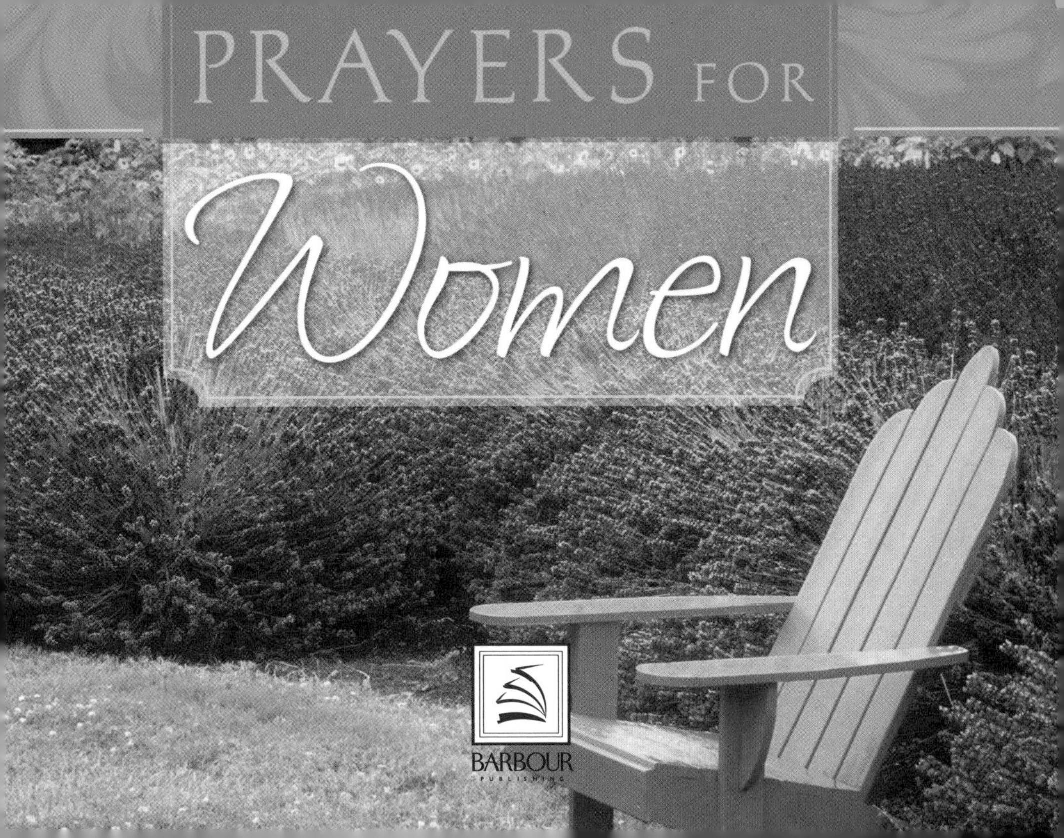
PRAYERS FOR
Women
BARBOUR
PUBLISHING

*Dear Father, thank You for my family.*
*I pray that You would bless them as they continue*
*to grow closer to You. Amen.*

*Lord, help me be the peacekeeper, never the one who stirs up more anger. Help me be an example to my whole family. Amen.*

*Father, protect my family from the evil one today.*
*Help them to keep their focus on You.*
*Amen.*

*Father, help me to be the woman that my family needs.*
*Show me how to love them more.*
*Amen.*

*When Your purpose is revealed to me,*
*Father, help me to accept my responsibility and do Your will.*
*Amen.*

*Submit yourselves, then, to God.*
*Resist the devil, and he will flee from you.*

JAMES 4:7 NIV

*I often feel that I lack faith, Lord, that You must be speaking promises for someone else—someone more faithful and deserving of them. Show me the error of this thinking. Amen.*

*Lord, I am human and often tempted.*
*Be with me when I am tempted and show me*
*the true joys of self-control. Amen.*

*Father, keep my family from temptation today. Help them to remember Your promise that You will always provide a way out. Amen.*

*Lord, I thank You for Your guidance and protection day after day. Although I never know what the day will bring, You have a plan, and I trust in You. Amen.*

*And without faith it is impossible to please God,*
*because anyone who comes to him must believe that he exists*
*and that he rewards those who earnestly seek him.*

Hebrews 11:6 NIV

*Father, when troubles come, I never have to face them alone. Thank You for always being with me as my refuge and strength. When all else fails, I put my trust in You and am never disappointed. Amen.*

*Lord, thank You for the ability to work—
at home and on the job. Let everything I do
be praise to You. Amen.*

*Precious Father, on my own, I am bound to fail. Now that I have put my trust in You, I cannot fail, for You are always the victor, and this knowledge makes me strong where once I was weak. Amen.*

*Lord, I want to help bring others to You, to be judged a virtuous woman for Your sake, not for any glory that might come to me. Use me as You see fit, because any work You give me is an honor. Amen.*

*When we are abandoned to God,*
*He works through us all the time.*

OSWALD CHAMBERS

*Lord, I want my house to be Your house—*
*a house of prayer, a place of comfort and peace, a refuge*
*to those in need. Help me make our home a blessing*
*for all who pass through its door. Amen.*

*Help me invest my time in more worthy pursuits, Lord, ones that will provide lasting satisfaction. I'm not sure what You will ask of me, but I am willing to try anything You recommend and give any resulting praise to You.*

*Amen.*

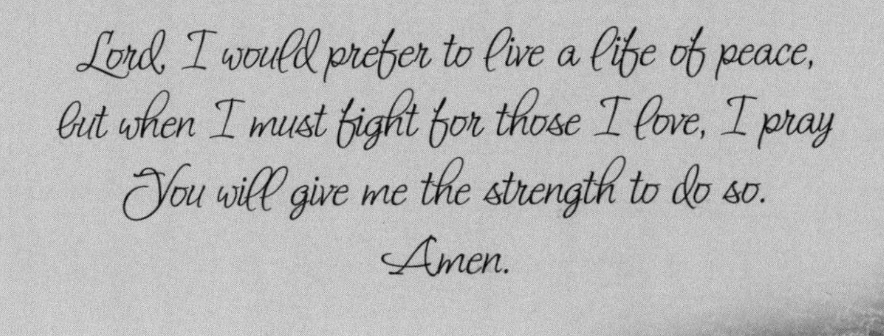

*Lord, I would prefer to live a life of peace,*
*but when I must fight for those I love, I pray*
*You will give me the strength to do so.*
*Amen.*

*Thank You, Father, for giving us all the things we need for life and godliness. You are the Great Provider. Amen.*

*Therefore if there is any encouragement in Christ, if there is any consolation of love, if there is any fellowship of the Spirit, if any affection and compassion, make my joy complete by being of the same mind, maintaining the same love, united in spirit, intent on one purpose.*

PHILIPPIANS 2:1–2 NASB

*Lord Jesus, draw my family close to You.*
*Fill our home with Your presence and our lives with Your love.*
*In turn, help each one of us to realize the importance*
*of blessing others. Amen.*

*Thank You, Lord, for being so faithful.*
*Thank You for Your compassion—that is just the right amount to get me through the day. Amen.*

*Lord, show me how to be a godly woman,*
*how to have true contentment that comes from service to You.*
*Help me to reinforce in my home the need to be*
*satisfied with doing Your will. Amen.*

*Lord, help me to rejoice in the time I have with my family today. I don't want to dwell on what might happen in the future; I want to relish this chance to nurture and cherish the blessings You've given me. Amen.*

*Yesterday is gone. Tomorrow has not yet come.*
*We have only today. Let us begin.*

Mother Teresa

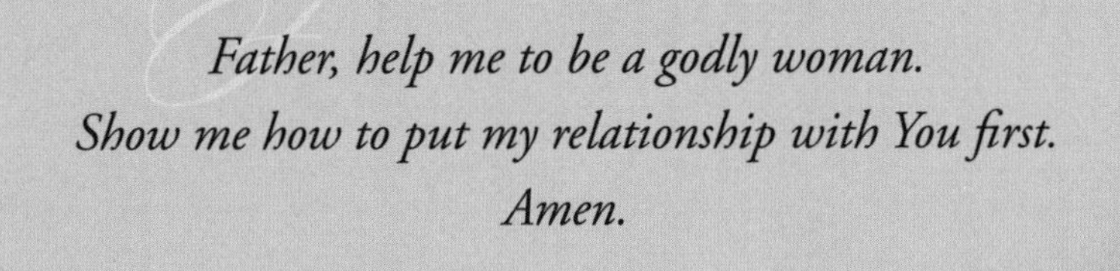

*Father, help me to be a godly woman.*
*Show me how to put my relationship with You first.*
*Amen.*

*Father, help me realize that my wants are temporary and of little importance. Let me lean against You, Lord, relaxed in the knowledge that You will care for me. Amen.*

*Father, I know my understanding is weak. But when I am in need of guidance, the first place I turn to is Your Word. Help me to search diligently, for I know the answers I need are there. Amen.*

*Blessed is the one who reads the words of this prophecy, and blessed are those who hear it and take to heart what is written in it, because the time is near.*

Revelation 1:3 NIV

*Lord, thank You for the blessing of my family.*
*Help me to not only tell them how much I love them each day,*
*but to show them as well. Amen.*

*Lord, thank You for every blessing, both big and small.*
*Help me to be more aware of the ways in which You take care of me,*
*so my gratitude can continue to grow. Amen.*

*Lord, if there's one thing I need, it's trustworthy guidance. In darkness or light, on fair days or foul, I trust that the light of Your Word will bring me safely home. Amen.*

*Lord, show me my errors and teach me the proper way to take advice. Amen.*

*Father, help me to learn to be sensitive to the needs of others.*
*Help me to show them Your love in every interaction.*
*Amen.*

*I have found the paradox that if I love until it hurts,*
*then there is no hurt, but only more love.*

MOTHER TERESA

*As for man, his days are like grass, he flourishes like a flower of the field; the wind blows over it and it is gone, and its place remembers it no more. But from everlasting to everlasting the LORD's love is with those who fear him, and his righteousness with their children's children—with those who keep his covenant and remember to obey his precepts.*

PSALM 103:15–18 NIV

*Lord, remove the fears that bind me so that I can be happy in the knowledge that You are there to comfort me—no matter what else is happening. Amen.*

*Lord, let me know when I am wrong. That way I can come to You for cleansing and an opportunity to make things right. Thank You for the truth in Your Word, even though sometimes the truth hurts. Amen.*

*Whatever you do, work at it with all your heart, as working for the Lord, not for men, since you know that you will receive an inheritance from the Lord as a reward. It is the Lord Christ you are serving.*

Colossians 3:23–24 NIV

*Lord, I need an attitude adjustment that can only come from You. Let me be a cheerful worker. Resolve my conflicted feelings, and give me Your peace. Amen.*

*Lord, I want to be instrumental in helping my family establish a close walk with You. Direct me daily to renew my commitment to follow in Your steps. Thank You for being the example I need. Amen.*

*Father, I need rest—rest from my schedule, rest from the demands of my family, rest from "doing" to a place of simply "being." Lead me to that place. Calm my mind and my emotions so I can slow down enough to find real rest. Amen.*

*Lord, I need Your gentle wisdom for every area of my life. I'm so thankful that what You offer is the best. Amen.*

*Because of Your strength, Lord, I can smile.*
*When I need peace, You strengthen me on the inside.*
*This is where I need You the most. Let me reflect Your strength*
*so that my children will be drawn to You also. Amen.*

*Get into the habit of saying, "Speak, Lord," and life will become a romance.*

Oswald Chambers

*Father, I get discouraged when I don't know which way to go. Remind me that You are right behind me, telling me which way to turn. Help me to be quiet and listen for Your guidance. Amen.*

*Father, I don't know how You will use my life,
but I have faith in Your promises and am always
ready to do Your will. Amen.*

*Forgive me, Lord, for those times when I've doubted Your love. Let me close my eyes, hold out my hand, and know that You are there. Thank You for being with me, Father. Amen.*

*Father, help me not to be a complaining woman. Fill my heart with joy over the tasks that I need to get done around the house. Amen.*

*Let there be kindness in your face, in your eyes, in your smile, in the warmth of your greeting. Always have a cheerful smile. Don't only give your care, but give your heart as well.*

J. S. Bach

*Lord, help me realize that my understanding is not necessary for the completion of Your plan. You understand everything; all I need to do is have faith. Amen.*

*Lord, when I see how You have interceded on my behalf,*
*I want to fall on my face before You. My prayers have been answered*
*in miraculous ways. In times when all I could see was darkness,*
*You provided light and power and hope. Amen.*

*There are times, Lord, when I feel as if You've forgotten me. How could I let those feelings of being forsaken overwhelm me? Help me to remember that the Creator of the entire universe holds me in His hands! Amen.*

*Thank You, Jesus, for Your sacrificial love for me. Thank You for the example of true love that You have provided. Amen.*

*I am the vine, you are the branches; he who abides in Me and I in him, he bears much fruit, for apart from Me you can do nothing.*

John 15:5 nasb

*Father, I need a reminder that what I should be is a servant.*
*I get so wrapped up in the need to maintain order that*
*I forget my job—to meet the needs of my family.*
*Please give me a servant's heart. Amen.*

*Father, I know the importance of spending quiet time with You in Your Word. Please place in my heart the urgency to be committed to my personal Bible study so that I can grow in You. Amen.*

*Father, I can't begin to count the number of times You've wrapped Your loving arms around me and calmed me in the midst of fears. You've drawn me near in times of sorrow and given me assurance when I've faced great disappointment. Amen.*

*Father, on days when I go off on my own, draw me close to You until I calm down and begin to think clearly. Everything is under control. All I need has been provided. Thank You. Amen.*

*For this reason a man will leave his father and mother and be united to his wife, and they will become one flesh.*

Genesis 2:24 NIV

*Lord, You know temptations surround me every day. Help me to avoid situations, places, and people that entice me to stray from Your will. Amen.*

*Lord, You are my hope in an often hopeless world. You are my hope of heaven, my hope of peace, my hope of change, purpose, and unconditional love. Fill the reservoir of my heart to overflowing with the joy that real hope brings. Amen.*

*Lord, show me the path to victory every day, because sometimes I find it hard to follow. You know every turn in the road, and I will follow You in security all the days of my life. Amen.*

*Lord Jesus, You have paid for my salvation through Your death on the cross; You made me a child of light, that I might guide others to You. You have made me worthy, and I thank You. Amen.*

*Every good and perfect gift is from above,*
*coming down from the Father of the heavenly lights,*
*who does not change like shifting shadows.*

James 1:17 niv

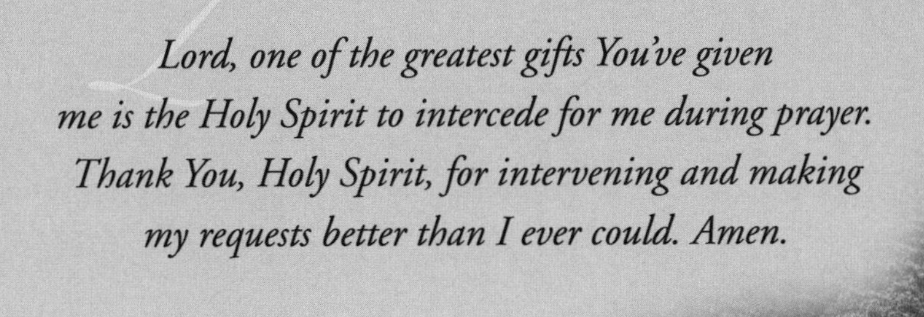

*Lord, one of the greatest gifts You've given me is the Holy Spirit to intercede for me during prayer. Thank You, Holy Spirit, for intervening and making my requests better than I ever could. Amen.*

*Father, help me to get over self-doubt.*
*Remind me that Your blessings are forever and*
*I have nothing to fear. Give me a merry heart.*
*Amen.*

*Father, as long as I trust in Your presence, I have nothing to worry about. Nothing can separate me from You, because You are the strong protector, the mighty One who watches over me always. I praise You, Lord, for Your protection. Amen.*

*Lord, on days when I'm having spiritual struggles, my thoughts become full of discouragement and frustration. I don't like to be so controlled by my emotions. Please give me the strength to be pure in every situation. Amen.*

*Therefore do not worry about tomorrow, for tomorrow will worry about itself. Each day has enough trouble of its own.*

MATTHEW 6:34 NIV

*Father, I want every moment of every day of my life to be a symphony of praise to You. Show me new ways to offer up worship to You today. Amen.*

*Lord, in the heat of anger, control my tongue,*
*because what I say then can be as damaging to my soul*
*as it is to my victim's reputation. Amen.*

*Lord, You stand before the throne of Your Father and claim me as Your own, exempt from sin and judgment. Because of Your sacrifice, I am made worthy. Thank You. Amen.*

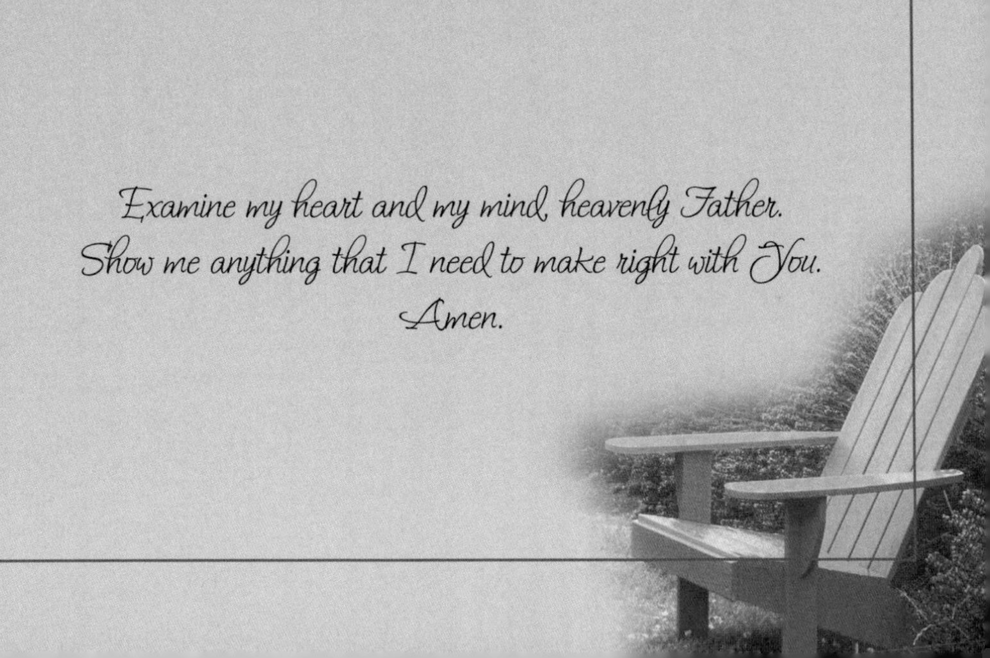

*Examine my heart and my mind, heavenly Father.*
*Show me anything that I need to make right with You.*
*Amen.*

*Jesus Christ is the same yesterday*
*and today and forever.*

HEBREWS 13:8 NIV

*Thank You for the times I am humbled, Lord. You are always here—to listen, to forgive, and to heal. Lord, help me to be repentant, to be willing to be brought low. Heal me, Lord. Amen.*

*Heavenly Father, we live in a world that lifts up proud people.*
*Make us all aware of how much You value sacrifice.*
*Help us to have the humble spirit we need*
*when we come before You. Amen.*

*Thank You, Jesus, for calling sinners to repentance.*
*If You had come only for the righteous,*
*I would not have been called, for I am a sinner.*
*I thank You for Your mercy. Amen.*

*Do nothing out of selfish ambition or vain conceit,*
*but in humility consider others better than yourselves.*

Philippians 2:3 NIV

*Whenever I feel pressure to exalt myself above others, Lord, remind me that my worth is found in You alone. Teach me to serve, to love, to be honest, to put the needs of others first— to live a humble but blessed life. Amen.*

*I know there are many things I cannot control, no matter how hard I may try, and many of life's events break my heart. Still I have hope, because through it all I have You. Thank You, Lord, for hope. Amen.*

*Let me tell thee, time is a very precious gift from God;*
*so precious that it's only given to us moment by moment.*

Amelia Barr

*But he said to me, "My grace is sufficient for you, for my power is made perfect in weakness." Therefore I will boast all the more gladly about my weaknesses, so that Christ's power may rest on me.*

2 Corinthians 12:9 NIV

*O Father, You have draped me in the garments of salvation and wrapped me snugly in the robe of righteousness. I am beautifully adorned by You—for You. You have given me all I need to live a joyful life, and I rejoice in Your gifts of beauty. Amen.*

*The meaning of prayer is that we get hold of God,*
*not of the answer.*

OSWALD CHAMBERS

*I tell You my problems and You listen, Lord. I speak of the good things in my life and You smile. I ask You for advice, knowing it will come in Your time. I am no longer lonely; I am loved. Amen.*

*You don't just notice me and pass on—*
*You actually take the time to think about me, pay attention to me,*
*help me when I need help, and protect me when I need protecting.*
*I am not alone. I am not forsaken. Thank You, Lord.*
*Amen.*

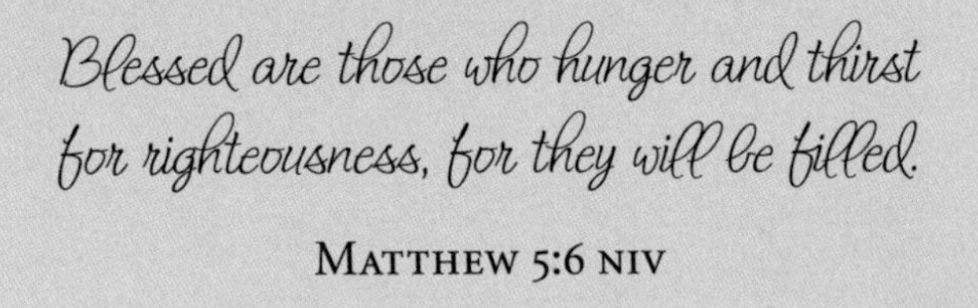

*Blessed are those who hunger and thirst for righteousness, for they will be filled.*

MATTHEW 5:6 NIV

*Father, make me mindful of Your great gifts,*
*that my song may praise Your work in my life. Amen.*

*Lord God, I put my hope in You for the situations I am in, for the hurts that afflict me, and for each second of my future. I trust in You that You will raise me up, just as You did Jesus. Amen.*

*Lord, sometimes I have to take a stand,*
*no matter what happens. When these times come,*
*I pray You will give me character and courage. Amen.*

*Lord, there is so much I do not understand about You.*
*Still, I can see the effects of Your actions,*
*the evidence that You are still active in my daily life.*
*I do not need to physically see You to believe.*
*Your evidence is everywhere. Amen.*

*Lord, I don't know if I'll ever understand why You sacrificed Yourself for me. But, from the depths of my being, I want to shout praises to You and also tell the whole world what You did for all of us. Amen.*

*I lift my soul to You and I trust in You, Lord.*
*Show me Your ways and teach me Your paths. Amen.*

*You love the short, the impaired, those who struggle with life and sometimes go under. You love me, Lord, so much that You call me forth by name and beautify me with Your salvation, the most precious ornament I could ever wish for. Amen.*

*Guard my life and rescue me, Father.
Help me to take refuge in You. Amen.*

*Father, I know that I tend to get focused on the negatives, and sometimes my thoughts are crowded with impatience, envy, anger, or resentment. Please help me focus on You. Fill me with pure thoughts. Amen.*

*Father, please be the center of my marriage.*
*Let our love be strong in You. Amen.*

*Turn Your ear to us, Father. Come quickly to our rescue.*
*Be the rock and refuge of our marriage. Amen.*

*For the eyes of the Lord are on the righteous and his ears are attentive to their prayer, but the face of the Lord is against those who do evil.*

1 PETER 3:12 NIV

*Lord, I really want to grow spiritually. I need to—for my own daily walk with You and, most importantly, because You've commanded me to. Thank You for giving me the strength to fulfill Your commands and to grow spiritually. Amen.*

*Father, Your Holy Spirit is telling me that self-control is not one of my strengths, and I need to work on it. I need temperance. Help me turn things over to You and allow You to develop self-control in my life. Amen.*

*Lord, there's so much chaos. Quiet my spirit.*
*Let me close my eyes for a moment and experience Your touch.*
*My strength comes from You, not from any other source. Calm me.*
*Keep me anchored in You and Your Spirit. Amen.*

*Thank You, God, for Your Word.*
*It instructs me how to live. It brings joy to my days*
*and gives me strength when I am weak.*
*Amen.*

*It is pleasing to God whenever thou rejoicest or laughest from the bottom of thy heart.*

MARTIN LUTHER

*You are like an army, Lord, surrounding me with Your strength and power. I don't have to depend on my limited might and abilities. Teach me to draw on Your strength. Amen.*

*The whole being of any Christian is Faith and Love. . . .*
*Faith brings the man to God, love brings him to men.*

MARTIN LUTHER

*Father, physically I'm wearing out. But in the core of my being, in my heart, I still feel strengthened by You. What a blessed promise that this inner strength will be my portion forever. Amen.*

*In the midst of suffering, I want to keep my eyes on You, Jesus. The suffering You endured for my sake makes my trials look like nothing. Help me look forward to the promise and to forget the temporary troubles I have now. Amen.*

*Father, help me understand faithfulness and to trust in Your love above all else, claiming none of Your glory as a personal reward. Amen.*

*Jesus. What a wonderful name!*
*It is the only name we need to call upon for salvation.*
*I praise You for being the way, the truth,*
*and the life, Lord. Amen.*

*Lord, I ask for Your help when it comes to getting along with my family members. Teach me to focus on the good times we had together, not the bad, and to concentrate on their good points for the sake of family peace. Amen.*

*Jesus, thank You for forgiveness. I know I'm not worthy of the grace You offer me every day. Please help me to never take Your gift for granted. Amen.*

*Father, Your correction lasts only a moment; but its blessings are eternal. When I realize You are so concerned for me and want to help me, I am filled with gratitude and willing to be led in the right direction. Amen.*

*Open your hearts to the love God instills. . . .
God loves you tenderly. What He gives you is not to
be kept under lock and key but to be shared.*

MOTHER TERESA

*Heavenly Father, my greatest responsibility as Your child is to share the gift of salvation with others. My family, my neighbors, my children—so many people need to hear Your Word. Make me attentive to each opportunity You present to me.*

*Amen.*

*Father, when my time on earth comes to an end,*
*I pray I will be able to bear death as well as I bore life,*
*secure in Your love and looking to the salvation that*
*You have promised is mine. Amen.*

*You bless my life in many ways every day, Father.
May I receive Your blessings with a song
of thanksgiving on my lips. Amen.*

*Lord, may those I work with see Your light shining through my life. Amen.*

*But the man who looks intently into the perfect law that gives freedom, and continues to do this, not forgetting what he has heard, but doing it—he will be blessed in what he does.*

JAMES 1:25 NIV

*Thank You for Your promise to guide me in all things great and small. Your eye is always on me, keeping me from error and ensuring that I can always find a way home to You. Amen.*

*When my time comes to grieve, Lord, be with me. Hold me up with Your mighty arms until I can stand on my own once more. Hasten the passing of my season of grief. Amen.*

*Lord, I do not know how to deliver myself from temptation, but You know the way. You have been there. When I stumble, I know Your arms will catch me; if I fall, You bring me to my feet and guide me onward. Amen.*

*Father, fill our hearts full of You and Your Word; then we can sing with grace and joy. My family and I can proclaim Your goodness to all those we meet. What a blessing! Amen.*

*Let other things come and go as they may,*
*let other people criticize as they will, but never allow anything*
*to obscure the life that is hid with Christ in God. Never be*
*hurried out of the relationship of abiding in Him.*

Oswald Chambers

*Jesus was blunt: "No chance at all if you think you can pull it off by yourself. Every chance in the world if you let God do it."*

MARK 10:27 MSG

*Lord, I know bad things will come my way in life, but I am secure in Your love that never fails. I am constantly blessed by Your care and concern. I am so important to You that even the hairs of my head are all numbered. Amen.*

*Lord, I want to learn to be patient and trust in You.*
*I know that You will hear my cries and I will*
*be blessed. Thank You for this blessing.*
*Amen.*

*Lord, I believe the call to motherhood comes from You. Help me approach my calling with a meek and humble spirit. Only when my outlook becomes Christlike will I truly be considered worthy of this calling. Amen.*

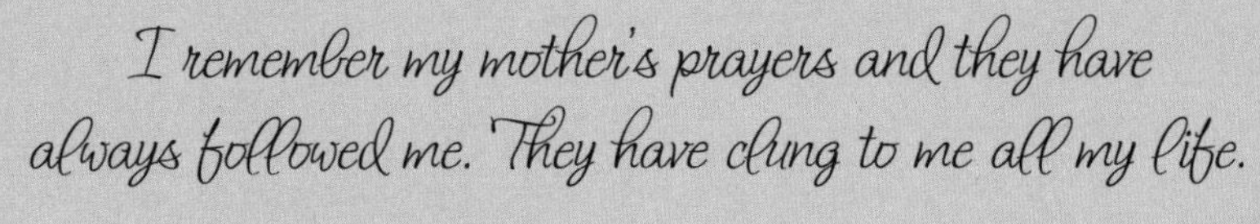

*I remember my mother's prayers and they have always followed me. They have clung to me all my life.*

Abraham Lincoln

*Father, help me to exalt You and praise Your name in my everyday life. Amen.*

*Father, when it comes to money matters,*
*I cannot approach perfection, but I know with Your help I can*
*learn to handle our family finances faithfully.*
*Amen.*

*Father, sometimes I have to go against the wishes of others to do Your will, and it's not always pleasant, but Your wishes come before all others, and I will do my best to honor Your name all my days. Amen.*

*Lord, I know that You are the one at work in me;*
*Your Spirit is a part of me, and You guide my thoughts and actions.*
*Thank You for that. I don't know what I would do if*
*I had to live life on my own. Amen.*

*God is never in a hurry.*

OSWALD CHAMBERS

*As I learn to rest in You, Lord, renew me.*
*Give me the ability I need to be patient, no matter what*
*trouble is around me. Let my joyful hope and*
*faithful prayers build up my patience.*
*Amen.*

*Father, help me to cast my cares on You,*
*knowing that You will sustain me. Amen.*

*Lord, direct me daily to accept and apply the strength that You've offered, so that I will truly have the gentle spirit that You intended me to have. Thank You, Jesus, that I don't have to do this on my own. Amen.*

*Father, quite often I pray for what is impossible.*
*But for You, nothing is impossible. Amen.*

*Lord, forgive me when I treat my family members poorly. Show me their good points, for I have overlooked or forgotten many of them. For the sake of our parents, our children, and ourselves, help me bring peace, forgiveness, and love to our family. Amen.*

*Father, help me remember that my priorities are not necessarily the priorities of those I love, so please give me the sense to step back and allow everyone a little leeway to lead their own lives. Help me be supportive, not bossy. Amen.*

*Lord, may I never hesitate to forgive anyone when You have already forgiven me. Amen.*

*Father, help me to have patience,*
*knowing my season is coming according to*
*Your timetable and trusting that with Your help,*
*every fruit I produce will be good. Amen.*

*Lord, sometimes compassion is all a person needs to gain strength. I pray I will always offer it freely. Amen.*

*Love all, trust a few, do wrong to none.*

William Shakespeare

*Through You, Lord, I can live a life that will give others no right to accuse me of any wrongdoing. I pray that You'll allow my life to be an example that will encourage my family, friends, and others to come to You. Amen.*

*Lord, help me overcome the urge*
*to pat myself on the back in the sight of others,*
*and wait to hear You say, "Well done." Amen.*

*Father, be with us today and stay near as we strive to raise our family in a way that will please You, and allow us to accomplish whatever You have planned. Amen.*

*Lord Jesus, help my husband and me*
*to trust and rest in Your unfailing love. Amen.*

*But when the Father sends the Advocate as my representative—that is, the Holy Spirit—he will teach you everything and will remind you of everything I have told you.*

John 14:26 NLT

*Lord, help me work to be a blessing to those around me in my daily life. Amen.*

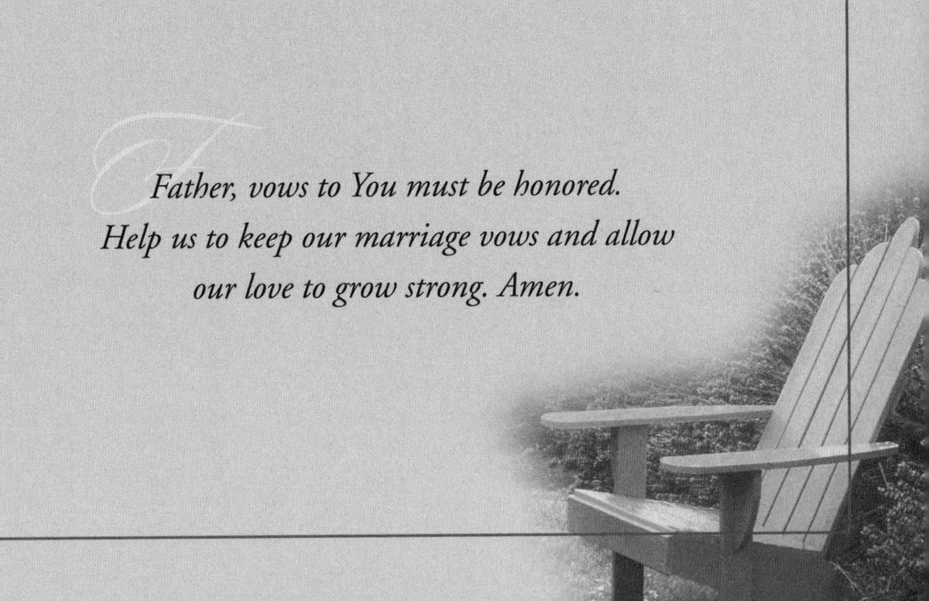

*Father, vows to You must be honored. Help us to keep our marriage vows and allow our love to grow strong. Amen.*

*Father, I admit that once in a while I have a temper tantrum, disputing Your guidance and wanting my own way, but You have never been wrong. Thank You for Your love and patience, for I will always need Your guidance. Amen.*

*Lord, help me give my family the aid and support they need. Amen.*

*Jesus, please bring new opportunities for God-filled relationships into my life today. I want You to use me to bless others and bring them closer to You. Amen.*

*Lord, give me the resolve to make things better,
to ignore my pride, and to do whatever is needed to
restore the harmony in my family. Amen.*

*Lord, help me to be charitable in all that I do.*
*My acts of charity reflect on You, and I want to*
*bring honor to You at all times.*
*Amen.*

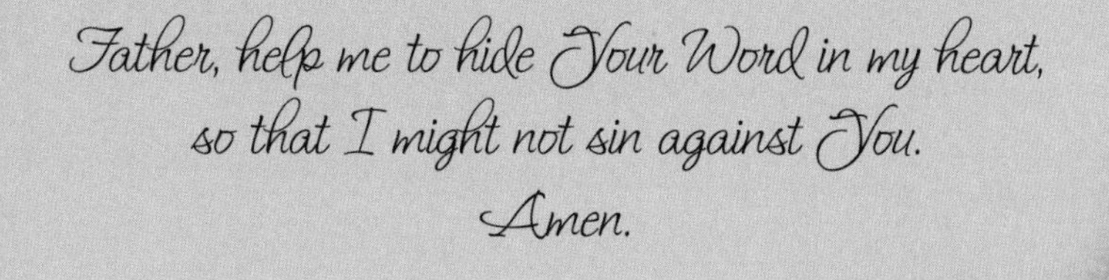

*Father, help me to hide Your Word in my heart,*
*so that I might not sin against You.*
*Amen.*

*Lord, help us to remember that You love us and You are faithful to all of Your promises. Amen.*

*Lord, I often make mistakes on the path of life,*
*losing sight of the trail and calling out for You.*
*Thank You for finding me, for putting my feet back on*
*the path and leading me home.*
*Amen.*

*We should come home from adventures, and perils,*
*and discoveries every day with new experience and character.*

HENRY DAVID THOREAU

*Lord, keep me on the right path when my own places are flawed, because only You know where You need me to be today and tomorrow. Amen.*

*Lord, help untangle my emotions and sort my jumbled thoughts. Calm my restless spirit. Help me experience Your supernatural peace in a real and tangible way. Amen.*

*Heavenly Father, I long for Your peace in my heart. Please take every anxious thread, every tightly pulled knot of uncertainty, sorrow, conflict, and disappointment into Your gentle, loving hands. Amen.*

*What hinders me from hearing is that I am taking up with other things. It is not that I will not hear God, but I am not devoted in the right place.*

Oswald Chambers

*Father, when happiness is hard to come by, help me to learn to draw more consistently on Your wellspring of joy. Help me delight in the little gifts You bring my way every day. Amen.*

*O God, help me think before I speak.*
*Put words of kindness in my mouth that will*
*build up others instead of destroying them.*
*I desire to be virtuous. Amen.*

*Father, teach me Your ways so that I can know You and find favor with You. Amen.*

*Lord, if I trust You for my eternal salvation,*
*why don't I trust You for my daily needs?*
*Instill in me the peace that comes from casting*
*all my cares on You. Amen.*

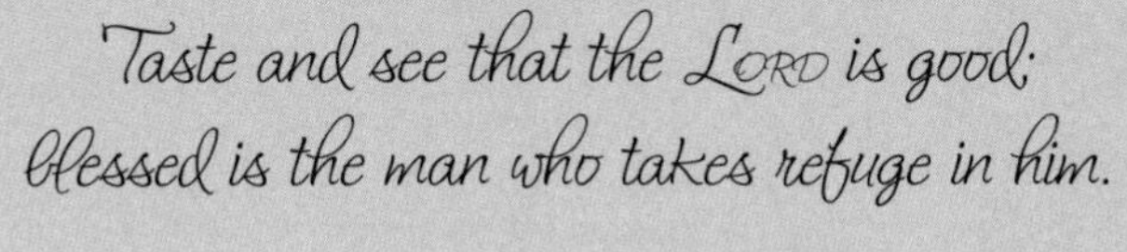

*Taste and see that the LORD is good;*
*blessed is the man who takes refuge in him.*

PSALM 34:8 NIV

*Lord, my life is full of distractions,
and I have too little time to absorb every sermon
the way I should. But You promise You will come
into my heart and live there if I welcome You.
Come into my heart, Lord Jesus. Amen.*

*Lord, the next time I am angry, guide me away from sin until I can speak words of peace and comfort once again. Amen.*

*Father, my heart is breaking. I need to know that You are near and that You care. Gently remind me that You have the power to heal every hurt, and help me make it through what I'm facing right now. Amen.*

*Father, every day is a battle.*
*I struggle between following You and choosing what feels right at the moment. I need Your wisdom and power to persevere toward a true change of heart and action.*
*But, most of all, I need Your forgiveness. Amen.*

*And we know that in all things*
*God works for the good of those who love him,*
*who have been called according to his purpose.*

Romans 8:28 niv

*Lord, I know I can't hope to escape every unpleasant circumstance in this world. Just the same, I will trust in You, whatever comes. Protect me in the way You see fit, in the way that best advances Your purposes for my life. Amen.*

*Lord, when it comes to courage,*
*I have none of my own. Without You, I would be*
*filled with fear, terrified of a future I cannot see.*
*Thank You for patiently taking my hand*
*and helping me face my fears. Amen.*

*Father God, though Your strength is limitless, it's tempered with wisdom and gentleness. You are both my strong tower and my tender, loving Father. Help me to find that proper balance of gentle strength in my own life. Amen.*

*Father, on my worst days I feel totally unworthy. But I know You have promised to cleanse me from all unrighteousness, to wipe away my guilt and make me whole if I confess my sins. Amen.*

*Father, give me Your peace and an understanding*
*that all things work together for good*
*when I follow Your will. Amen.*

*Lord, life seems overwhelming to me sometimes.*
*Please give me the abundant wisdom You've promised,*
*and help me to relax in the knowledge that*
*You will guide me. Amen.*

*Father, You have given us Your Word and Your Holy Spirit to teach us. Help me to seek You each day. Amen.*

*Lord, as I read and study Your Word and hear sermons preached about it, I still have questions and much to learn. I ask that You give me a clear understanding of what You are saying to me through it. Amen.*

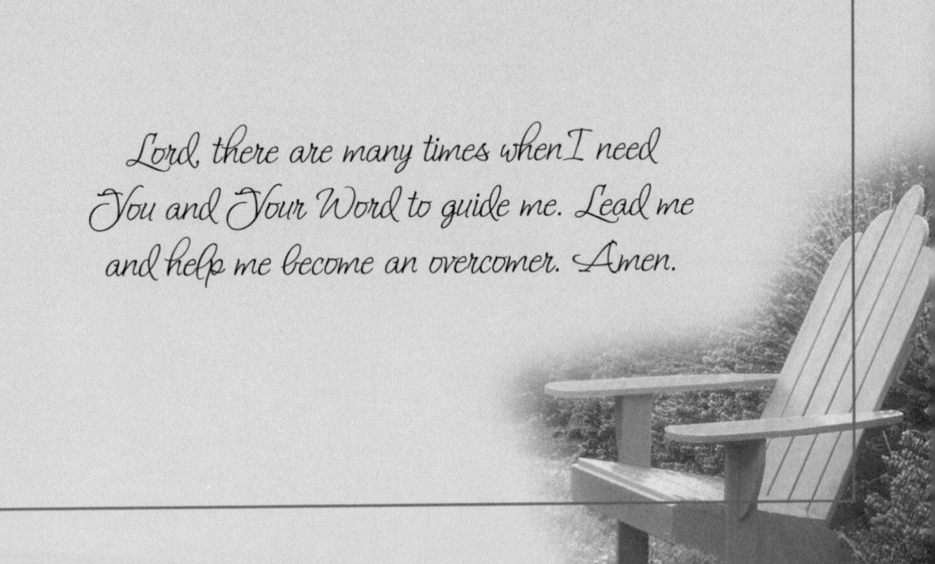

*Lord, there are many times when I need You and Your Word to guide me. Lead me and help me become an overcomer. Amen.*

*Thank You, Lord, for Your love and faithfulness to us. Thank You for making us Your people, for allowing us to be the sheep of Your pasture. Thank You for allowing us to serve such a great God! Amen.*

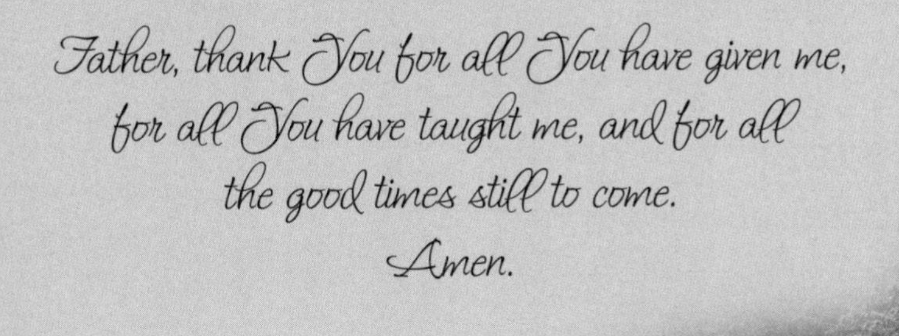

*Father, thank You for all You have given me,*
*for all You have taught me, and for all*
*the good times still to come.*
*Amen.*